Let's go to
THAILAND

Keith Lye

General Editor
Henry Pluckrose

Franklin Watts

London   New York   Sydney   Toronto

Facts about Thailand

Area:
514,000 sq. km.
(198,457 sq. miles)

Population:
53,223,000 (1986 estimate)

Capital:
Bangkok

Largest cities:
Bangkok (5,468,000)
Chiang Mai (105,000)
Nakhon Ratchasima
   (87,000)
Khon Kaen (80,000)
Udon Thani (76,000)

Official language:
Thai

Religion:
Buddhism (95 percent)

Main exports:
Rice, tapioca products,
rubber, tin, maize, sugar

Currency;
Baht

Franklin Watts Limited
12a Golden Square
London W1

ISBN: UK Edition 0 86313 336 3
ISBN: US Edition 0 531 10106 1
Library of Congress Catalog
Card No: 85 51578

© Franklin Watts Limited 1986

Typeset by Ace Filmsetting Ltd,
Frome, Somerset
Printed in Hong Kong

Maps: Tony Payne
Design: Arthur Brown
Stamps: Stanley Gibbons Limited
Photographs: Zefa; Tourist Authority of
Thailand, 9, 10, 19, 20, 31; Neil
Thomson, 8, 16, 24, 26, 27, 28; Paul
Forrester, 12
Front cover: Zefa
Back cover: Zefa

Thailand is a monarchy in Southeast
Asia. It is a little larger than Spain.
About 95 out of every 100 people are
Buddhists. The Wat Phra Keo (the
Temple of the Emerald Buddha) in
Bangkok is the Royal Temple, where
the king performs his religious duties.

Chiang Mai, the second largest city, is in a mountain valley in Thailand's northern highland region. Here a group of farmers takes part in a parade before their king. Chiang Mai, which was founded in 1296, is famed for its many handicraft shops.

In the northern mountains many houses are built on stilts. They give people protection against snakes, especially in the rainy season which lasts from June to October. Thailand is a tropical country. The south is hot throughout the year.

The fertile Central Plain lies between the northern highlands and the sea coast around the Gulf of Thailand. About 83 out of every 100 people live in villages in country areas. Most farmers have small plots of land.

Many rivers flow from the northern mountains across the Central Plain. The chief river, the Chao Phraya, enters the Gulf of Thailand just south of Bangkok. Many farmers sell their produce at floating river markets.

Bangkok has many temples. The oldest and largest, Wat Po, contains the Reclining Buddha, a statue 46 m (151 ft) long and 15 m (49 ft) high. It is covered with gold leaf. The picture shows part of this huge statue.

Pattaya is a resort of the shore of the Gulf of Thailand, southeast of Bangkok. A few years ago it was a tiny fishing village. It now attracts many foreign tourists, who enjoy various water sports, such as "para-sailing".

Southwestern Thailand consists of a long, narrow finger of land, called a peninsula. Thailand shares this land with Burma and Malaysia. Phuket is a popular resort on Thailand's largest island, also called Phuket, which lies off the west coast of the peninsula.

Phang Nga Bay is northeast of Phuket. This beautiful inlet is dotted with rocky islets, which have been undercut by the waves. There are many strange limestone caves. Part of a James Bond movie called "The Man with the Golden Gun" was made here.

The picture shows some stamps and money used in Thailand. The main unit of currency is the baht, which is divided into 100 stangs.

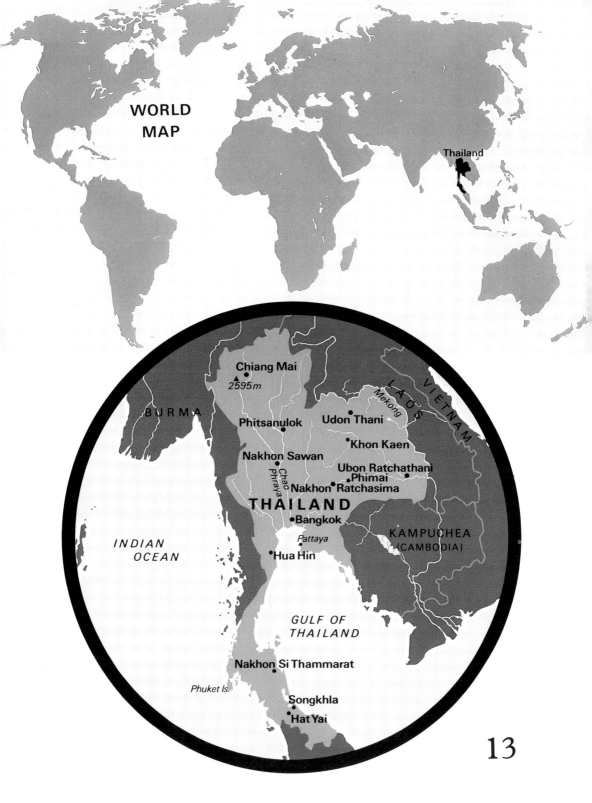

WORLD
MAP

Thailand

Chiang Mai
▲ 2595m

BURMA

Phitsanulok

Udon Thani

Khon Kaen

Nakhon Sawan

Ubon Ratchathani
Phimai
Nakhon Ratchasima

LAOS

VIETNAM

Mekong

Chao Phraya

THAILAND

Bangkok

Pattaya

INDIAN
OCEAN

Hua Hin

KAMPUCHEA
(CAMBODIA)

GULF OF
THAILAND

Nakhon Si Thammarat

Phuket Is.

Songkhla

Hat Yai

13

The ancestors of the Thais probably came from southern China. They founded the first Thai kingdom in 1238. Its capital was near the modern city of Phitsanulok in the north. Bangkok became the capital in 1782. Shown here is the Grand Palace in Bangkok.

14

The picture shows a procession of royal barges on the Chao Phraya River in Bangkok. Between 1782 and 1939, Thailand was called Siam. Its official name today is Muang Thai. This means Land of the Free.

The king is Head of State, but the prime minister heads the government. The National Assembly, which consists of a Senate and an elected House of Representatives, selects the prime minister. The National Assembly building, seen here, is in Bangkok.

16

Bangkok is a mixture of old and new buildings. It was a tiny village until 1782, but it is now Thailand's leading commercial, cultural and industrial city. It is also the seat of government. Its local name is Krung Thep. This name is Thai for City of Angels.

The Khmer people of Kampuchea (Cambodia) once dominated eastern Thailand. Impressive ruins of Khmer cities, such as this one at Phimai in the northeast, can still be seen. Thai forces invaded Kampuchea in 1431 and seized its capital, Angkor.

Ayutthaya, which is about 70 km (43 miles) north of Bangkok, was founded in 1350. It became the second capital of the Thai kingdom, but the Burmese destroyed it in 1767. It was replaced as capital by Thon Buri. Thon Buri is now part of the city of Bangkok.

Farming, the main activity, employs 76 out of every 100 workers. The chief crop is rice, shown here at harvest time. Thailand, one of Southeast Asia's more prosperous countries, is the fifth largest rice producer.

Only 90 years ago, the main forms of transport were river boats, elephants and ox-drawn carts. Although river transport still remains important in the interior, Thailand now has one of Southeast Asia's best rail and road systems.

Forests cover about three-fifths of Thailand. Valuable teak and other trees are cut down and elephants drag the logs out of the forest, where they are floated downstream to sawmills. Rubber is another forest product.

Water buffalo are important and many farmers use them to work the flooded and muddy ricefields. Water buffalo love being in water, especially on blazing hot afternoons when their owners are resting indoors.

Fishing in the Gulf of Thailand and in the many rivers and ponds inland is an important activity. Fish, often served with a spicy sauce, is a popular food. These fishing boats are moored at Hua Hin, a port and resort which is southwest of Bangkok.

Industry employs 9 out of every 100 people. Thailand ranks fourth in world tin production and it has other minerals. Handicrafts, such as pottery, are made by skilled workers. Other manufactures include cement, food products, textiles, wood and paper.

Children between the ages of 7 and 14 must attend free, government-run elementary schools. About one-third of pupils then go on to secondary or vocational schools. Most secondary schools are privately owned.

In country areas, many children have to travel long distances to school by bus. Education has increased greatly in recent years. By the early 1980s, about 86 out of every 100 adults could read and write. Thai children know that the future of their country depends on education.

Buddhism was founded in India about 2,500 years ago. The influence of the Buddha is clear everywhere in Thailand, where monks wearing yellow robes are common sights. This picture shows children at school learning to meditate in order to seek truth.

Wealthy Thai families live in modern homes and wear western clothes. Their comfortable life contrasts with that of many villagers. Outside the cities, the traditional panung, a cotton or silk garment wrapped tightly around the body, is the common dress.

Many young people enjoy kite fighting contests. The aim is to use your kite to knock your opponent's kite out of the sky. Thai-style boxing is another unusual sport, because boxers can use both their hands and bare feet to strike their opponent.

Thais are known as gentle and lighthearted people. They love music and dance. Some dances tell stories from Buddhist and Hindu books. This picture shows a dancing troupe. Here the dancers must avoid getting their feet trapped between the painted poles.

Index